T0380874

CLEO,
The Curious Cat

Little Nickel

Copyright © 2010 by Little Nickel. 532759

Library of Congress Control Number: 2010912329

ISBN: Softcover   978-1-4535-6175-1
         Hardcover   978-1-4535-6176-8

Print information available on the last page

Rev. date: 05/13/2019

To order additional copies of this book, contact:
Xlibris
1-888-795-4274
www.Xlibris.com
Orders@Xlibris.com

Preface

Cleo came into my life when I was very lonely. I had just lost my family and friends.

Cleo was a very special friend. She was my companion. She showed me lots of LOVE.

From the day Cleo arrived at my front door, we never parted.

Cleopatra Sirocco was a very special cat.

Acknowledgment

I would like to thank Dr. Mark Evens, a special friend that gave me a lot of encouragement, and Cortney Nickel, my granddaughter, for her great graphics.

Her story starts when she arrived at my front door.

So, this is my new home. WOW! It's big! It sparkles!

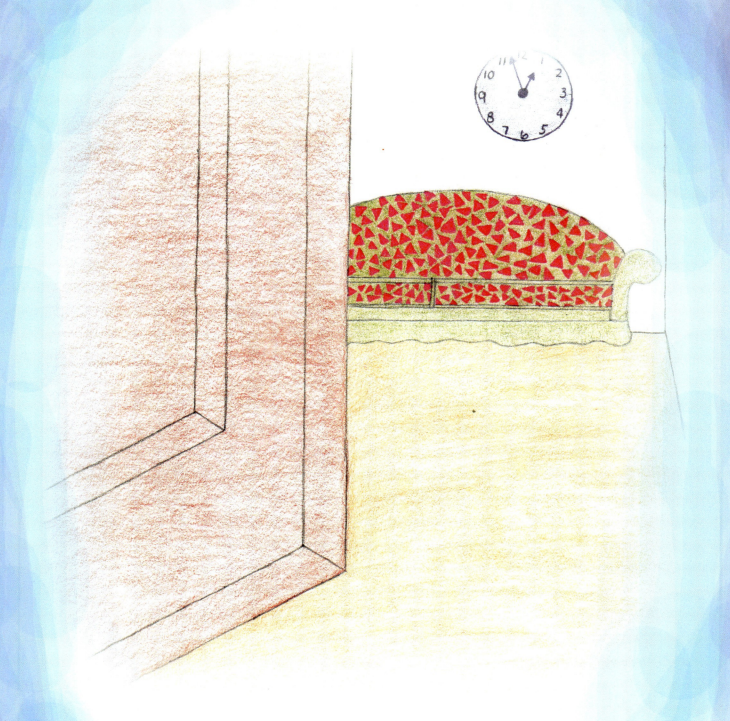

There is a door. Open the door. Why doesn't someone open the door? Here comes my big chance.

What is this? It is not grass. Ouch! It hurts my feet! Nobody told me there would be pine needles. I will just tip toe. *HOLD IT.* What is that long and thin. I will catch one and take it home to Ma.

Ma, I have a gift for you.

"Oh Cleo! How nice, but let's put him
back outside with his friends."

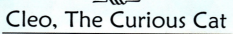

I don't understand. Ma picks me up and loves me. That is all I need. That made everything OK.

I am going to be very happy here. I jumped into bed with Ma. Boy, I was tired. The trip was very stressful and I had no time to take a nap today.

Ma was in service in Florida. We were there for six months.

I was looking out a big window and all I could see was water,
a pool and grass. How do I get down to the ground?
I will find a way down, later.

Who is coming in the door? It is Aunt Penny! Good, she will
let me out. Aunt Penny lets me out for a run
every morning. I love my Aunt Penny!

One morning I visited a disabled neighbor named Maude. After many hours of giving a lot of love to me, they found my telephone number on my collar tag. After calling Ma, Aunt Penny came to pick me up. I was still on Maude's lap.

They loved me so much, that they wanted to keep me. Ma loved me too much for that. Ma was so glad to see me.

Later I brought a toad in for Aunt Penny. It was funny to see Aunt Penny jumping all over the place, trying to catch the toad.

Christmas

Tina our cleaning lady came today. I was sleeping when
I heard the doorbell ring. I jumped up to go to the door.
There's Tina! Tina picked me up and said "Hello, Miss Cleo.
Are you ready to go out?" I sat and waited for the door to
open to go outside. OH, I missed the door. Finally I looked at
Tina and said" OUT! OUT!"

What 's that? Tina is putting a tree up, just for me.
Tina had the tree decorated. It was beautiful!

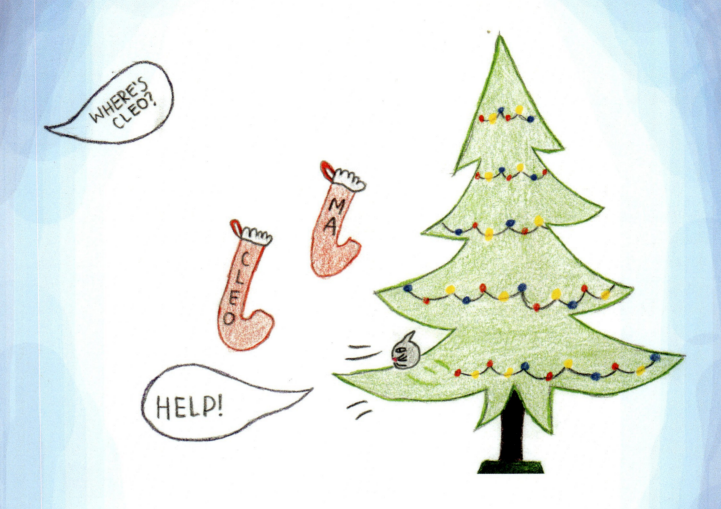

Tina called out to Ma. "The tree is moving!"
She spread the branches of the tree apart and
there I was!" OUT! OUT!"

It was a great Christmas with Ma, family, friends and me.

Jozelyn is one year old. She came to visit me.
I fell in love with her right away.

"Here comes Joselyn?" She puts her head on mine
and said I love you.

Joselyn is so loveable. She throws the ball to me and
I take it back to her. She would play with my toys.

It was time for Joselyn's nap. So I lay down on
the pillow beside her crib

Today she is going home. She said good bye and I
told her I loved her very much.

Cleopatra Sirocco

Cleo was very much loved by me and everyone that knew her.

In September 2009, she became ill with cancer, for which there was no cure. It has taken me a long time to recover from Cleo's death. A part of her will always be with me.

After realizing how much it costs to care for a sick pet, I decided to write this in memory of my best friend and dedicate it to Cleo and all of my grandchildren.

For every book that sells, I will donate 10 percent cost of book to an organization that helps with the costs of cats and rights of cats.

Printed in the United States
By Bookmasters